my valentine

luna osho

my valentine

illustrated by the author

a collection of love poems

copyright © 2024 by luna osho

all rights reserved. no part of this book may be used or reproduced in any manner whatsoever without written permission except in the case of reprints in the context of reviews.

first edition - january 2024

cover design: luna osho

isbn: 979-8877178779

this book is dedicated to the one i love
thank you for everything

contents

i love you   9

about the author   88

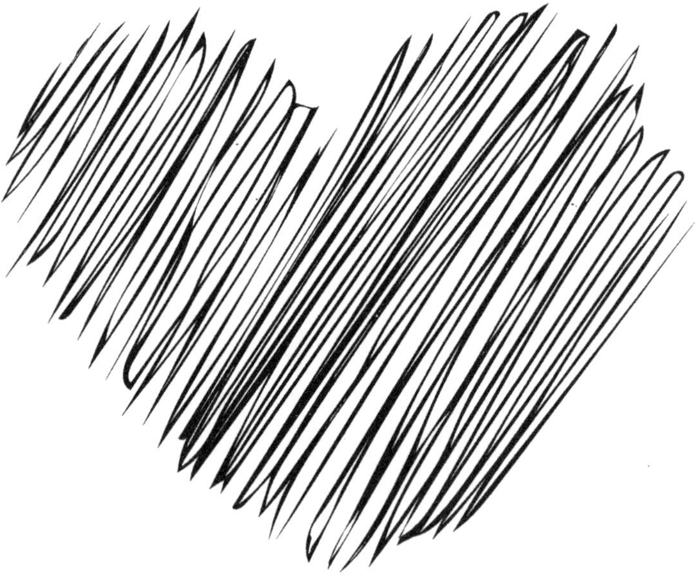

i love you

we are like the seasons
our love ebbs and flows
our love waxes and wanes
our love rises and falls

yet our love remains

like the sea that beats upon the shore
and the waves that wash away the sand
like the leaves that fall from the trees
and the grass that grows anew in the spring

our love remains

never-ending

eternal

my valentine

we are fire

you and i

we melt together

we are hot

we are bright

we burn everything away

a million years

could not have been

enough

to measure

the love

i have for you

my valentine

we

will love each other

till the end of time

just you and i

always and forever

you are my love

the fire in my heart

my light in the dark

you are my heart and soul

my love

my reason to go

my valentine

we are two halves

complementary

you are the day

i am the night

together we are one

complete

happy

i love you my dear

from the depths of my heart

never forget

that i love you

my valentine

i want you to love me
to need me
like i need you

i want you to trust me
to love me
like i love you

my love for you is pure
unfettered and uninhibited

i would endure any hardship
and overcome any obstacle

to keep you safe
i'll be at your side

my valentine

we are inseparable

and always will be

you are my sunshine
my beautiful blue sky

without you

there would be no light
to illuminate my world

my valentine

how can i describe your beauty?

the beauty of your soul?

how can i see

the essence of you?

how can i show

your light

is the beacon of my life?

you are my strength

when i have to be brave

the reason

for me to pave

a path of joy and love

my valentine

there is a light

in your eyes

and a fire in your soul

like the sun

so radiant

so clear

but it is

your smile

that has filled my world

with a brilliant glow

luna osho

i hope i will be

the source of your joy

the river to feed your love

my valentine

you know i would give you the world

love you till the end of time

love you forever

be your safe harbor

always take care of you

that's my vow

you are the one i run to
the one i trust the most
with my heart and life
you are the one i count on

you are my rock
my strength
and my courage

when i need you most
and no matter what happens
or what we may face
you will always be the one

my valentine

we may be not

the perfect couple

but we are perfect for us

that's enough

your eyes are so beautiful

like a mirror

reflecting your inner thoughts and feelings

like an open book

i can look into every page

your soul is bare

and i see into its depths

your heart is pure

and i hear its song

you are truly

beautiful

my valentine

your love is my shelter

my sanctuary

it is the place where i can go

when the world becomes too much

your love is my solace

my respite

it is the place where i can hide

from the pain

your love is my home

my haven

it is the place where i feel safe

where i feel loved

you are my best friend
my lover and my muse

you are the music in my soul
you are the reason i write

without you
i would have no life
my darling
my dearest
my love

without you
i would have no life

my valentine

your love is the only thing

to keep me going

it is the only thing

that drives me

your love is the only thing

that gives meaning

to mine

we have become

a single entity

joined together

by our love

and our commitment

to each other

we have become

as one

forever

and ever

my valentine

love is the answer

it is the cure

the key

the light

the way

the one thing

we all need

to survive

to live

to breathe

to thrive

our love

our friendship

and our understanding of each other

grow deeper

every day

my valentine

we have seen

both the worst and the best

of each other

and yet

here we are

still standing together

still loving each other

if we can

stand the test of time

through all the trials and tribulations

that life has thrown at us

then we can stand the test of anything

together

and nothing can tear us apart

when i think of you

the stars themselves shine brighter

when i think of you

the oceans churn and boil

when i think of you

the earth itself trembles

for you

i would move mountains

for you

i would wage war

and for you

i would face death itself

my valentine

you have changed my life

in a million ways

and for that

i love you

there are many ways
to express love

some are quiet
and some are loud

some are gentle
and some are wild

but they all have
the same thing in common

all are forms of love

my valentine

i will love you

through good times and bad times

when the sun is shining

and the rain is pouring

when the wind is blowing

and the air is still

i will love you

for the rest of my life

and even when i am gone

my love for you will remain

long after my soul will leave this world

for our love is eternal

sometimes

a word can convey so much

sometimes

a simple glance is enough

sometimes

the silence speaks louder than anything

sometimes

we don't need to talk

because words cannot express
what we are feeling

sometimes

words aren't necessary

because what we share
is always love

my valentine

you are like an ocean

deep and mysterious

with countless secrets

that i want to explore

what can i say

except

that i love you

what can i do

except

tell you

that i will never leave you

what can i give

except

my heart

for you to keep

what can i offer

except

to be with you

until death do us part

my valentine

my love

i have one request

stay with me

don't go

let me be with you

forever

my heart

will never forget you

and neither will my mind

for you have left a permanent mark

on every cell of my body

you will remain in my heart

until the day i die

and perhaps even after that

your soul is a part of mine

now and forever

my valentine

the words i write to you

are a reflection of my soul

my feelings for you

are a mirror to my heart

so please

read these words

and know the depth of my love

for you

every poem

is a love letter

each page

a gift

to you

the one

i cherish

my valentine

any moment i spend
with you is a blessing
and i am eternally grateful
for your love

my beautiful angel
thank you for making my life
so much better
than it was yesterday

your touch

sets me on fire

because you are a miracle

a gift

from heaven

my valentine

your kiss

is like a rose

and your body

my garden

when i'm with you

i feel

more alive

than i've ever been

i love how

i feel so calm around you

i love how

you can make me smile

no matter what i'm feeling

i love how

you listen to me

even when i'm rambling

i love how

we can talk for hours

about anything

everything

nothing

my valentine

our love

is a wonderful tree

standing strong

and tall

against the elements

and it is all thanks

to you

my love

for helping me

plant that seed

all those years ago

you are my light

my hope

my inspiration

you are my life

my home

my destination

you are the reason

i get up each day

and face the world

with a smile to stay

you are the one

who makes my heart sing

and my life worth living

i will love you

forever

and ever

my valentine

when you are down
i will be there
to lift you up

when you are hurt
i will be there
to comfort you

when you are afraid
i will be there
to ease your mind

whenever you need
i will be there
and will never
leave
you

look into my eyes

and see the world

as you want it to be

for that is what i see

when i look into yours

take my hand

feel my heart

beat

my valentine

i would give you everything
from the air in my lungs
to the blood in my veins
until i become part of you
and you of me

for you give me all i need
and i need to give you all i have

for loving me

the sun

is warm

yet you

are warmer

my valentine

your touch

makes my skin

tingle

your voice

makes my mind

whirl

your smile

makes my heart

flutter

you are the light of my life

my dream to live

when i am with you

nothing else matters

my valentine

you have my love

because you are you

because you have

your beautiful eyes

your wonderful smile

and your brilliant mind

your heart

your love

are more than i need

so how could i ask for

anything else

when i already

have everything

my valentine

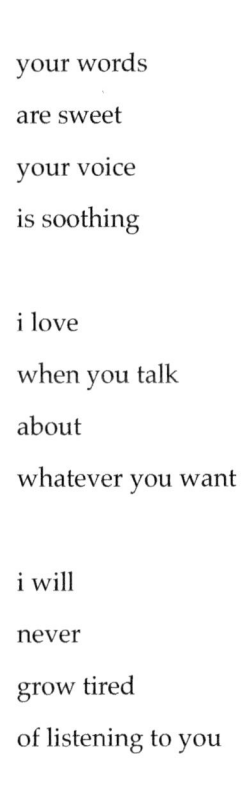

your words

are sweet

your voice

is soothing

i love

when you talk

about

whatever you want

i will

never

grow tired

of listening to you

my love

when we're together

you give me a reason

to keep on living

because without you

the world would be so gray

my valentine

i love you

more than words

can say

let me hold your hand
as we walk along the sand
or ride the wind together
upon the eagle's back

let me whisper to you
in the silence of the stars
as we lie upon the hill
and look up to the sky

let me be your warmth
your strength
your solace
for now and forever

my valentine

if i had to choose only one thing

to take from this world

i would take you

the one i love most

because life would not be complete

without you

let our love

outshine the sun

and the moon

and the stars

and everything else in this universe

and let it

never

die

my valentine

i'm yours

and you're mine

that's how we were meant to be

we are two

in one

there are a thousand ways to love you
and a thousand ways for me to show it
whether by holding your hand
or just listening when you speak

there are a million ways to love you
and a million ways for me to show it
whether by kissing your lips
or just watching you sleep

there are infinite ways to love you
and i will do my utmost to show them all

my valentine

there is no greater joy

than waking up next to you

your smile is beautiful

i am lucky to have you in my life

it feels like

we were

alone

in the world

just you and me

no one else

nothing

but us

together

in love

my valentine

if this is a dream

please don't wake me

i don't want this moment

to end

luna osho

i can see the stars

and the moon

and the whole universe

when you look at me

my valentine

sometimes

you need a hug

sometimes

a kiss

but often

it's better to say nothing

and just

be there

if we had met

in a different time

a different place

would our hearts

still beat as one?

yesss

my valentine

you complete me
like no one else can
and my life is bright
when you are at my side

your touch

is warm

and comforting

you can calm me down

just by

holding my hand

you're so gentle

so caring

so sweet

my valentine

when i look into your eyes

i see
a galaxy
of emotions

i don't understand

how
one person
can be
so complex

but i'm willing
to figure it out

luna osho

i'm glad
i found you

and
you

found
me

my valentine

there's a world of people

out there

and you're here

with me

we found our home
our love
our everything

we found each other
and our home is not a place
it is a feeling
an emotion
and it is love

we will grow old
we will grow strong
we will grow together

always

my valentine

when the sky

is full of clouds

it's nice to have someone

who can chase them away

we've been through a lot

and we're not done yet

together

we can make it

because

i'm not going

anywhere

without you

and you

are not

leaving

without me

my valentine

i could

not have

manifested

anything

more

beautiful

than

you

you're perfect

just the way you are

don't ever

let anyone tell you otherwise

you're perfect

to me

and that's all

that matters

my valentine

every word

you speak

is poetry

it flows

like a stream

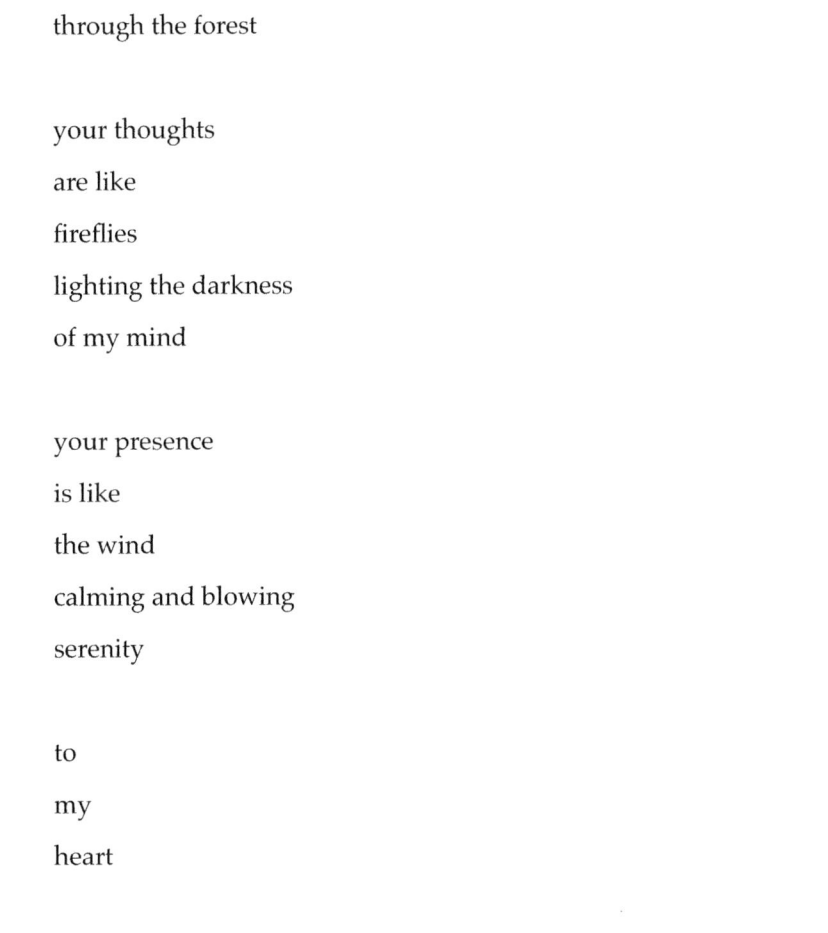

through the forest

your thoughts

are like

fireflies

lighting the darkness

of my mind

your presence

is like

the wind

calming and blowing

serenity

to

my

heart

i remember

how our love started

it was like a tiny seed

germinating and growing

into a beautiful flower

and today

after years of nurturing

our love has bloomed

into a wonderful garden

full of life and beauty

and i wouldn't trade it

for the world

my valentine

the sun has set

and the moon has risen

and so it is time

for me to go to bed

but i will leave you

with one last gift

one last present

my heart

i know

you will enjoy it

as much as

i did

creating it

so

without further ado

here it is

the

final

piece

in my

valentine's

expression

of love

about the author

luna osho is an aspiring poet who has chosen to be anonymous. she currently lives in a remote part of france with her beloved cat. she loves poetry, cinema, travel, and books. when she's not writing or reading, she enjoys watching films or visiting art museums. her dream is one day to become a full-time author while living and traveling all around the world. you can find out more about her on tiktok and instagram: @luna.osho

Printed in Great Britain
by Amazon